*To my grandchildren, Daniel and Benjamin, with love*

Published by
**Lion Publishing plc**
Sandy Lane West, Oxford, England
ISBN 0 7459 1951 0
**Lion Publishing Corporation**
1705 Hubbard Avenue, Batavia, Illinois 60510, USA
ISBN 0 7459 1951 0
**Albatross Books Pty Ltd**
PO Box 320, Sutherland, NSW 2232, Australia
ISBN 0 7324 0473 8

First edition 1991

**Acknowledgments**
The words of the following carols are copyright and are included by kind permission of the copyright holders.
Michael Perry, 'Gabriel the Angel Came', 'See Him Lying on a Bed of Straw', 'When Shepherds Watched and
Angels Sang', copyright © Michael Perry/Jubilate Hymns. For USA: reprinted by permission of Hope Publishing
Company, Illinois. Timothy Dudley-Smith, 'Donkey Plod and Mary Ride', 'Holy Child', 'Within a Crib', 'How
Faint the Stable Lantern's Light', 'The Shining Stars Unnumbered', 'Not in Lordly State and Splendour', 'Stars of
Heaven Clear and Bright', 'A Song was Heard at Christmas', 'Come Now with Awe', copyright © Timothy
Dudley-Smith. For USA: reprinted by permission of Hope Publishing Company, Illinois. S. Stevens, 'The Colours
of Christmas', copyright © S. Stevens.

The Christmas story, retold on pages 13, 29, 45 by Timothy Dudley-Smith, is from *Stories of Jesus* published by
Lion Publishing.

Special thanks to Chris Kipling for the musical arrangements and to Francis Robson for preparing the score script.

The compiler's royalties on this book go to the Orchard Vale Trust, communities for the mentally
handicapped (Registered Charity Number: 326940).

**British Library Cataloguing in Publication Data**
  A Song at Christmas
  1. Christmas carols in English
  I. Absolon, Mary II. Morris, Tony
  782.5280942
  ISBN 0 7459 1951 0

**Library of Congress Cataloging-in-Publication Data**
  —1st ed.
  ISBN 07459 1951 0
  I. Carols. 2. Christmas Music
  I. Absolon, Mary. II. Morris, Tony, ill.
  PZ8.3.C199 1991
  808.81'933—dc20

Printed and bound in Singapore

# A Song at Christmas

Compiled by Mary Absolon

Illustrations by Tony Morris

Story retellings by Timothy Dudley-Smith

A LION BOOK

Oxford · Batavia · Sydney

# Contents

# Gabriel the Angel Came

Gabriel the angel came
    to greet the virgin Mary:
'Peace' he said, and called her name,
'For joyful news I carry:
the Lord of all from realms above
has looked upon your soul in love:
you shall give birth
to Christ on earth,
the Saviour;
you bear the hope of grace—
and mark of heaven's favour,
and all shall see God's face.'

Mary asked 'How can it be;
my love is given to no one,
and Joseph is betrothed to me—
can what is done be un-done?'
'The Spirit comes—and this is how
God's power will be upon you now:
Don't be afraid,
what God has said
will cheer you—
the promise is not in vain—
all people shall revere you,
and virtue shall remain.'

Mary then with joy replied
'I serve the Lord of Heaven:
to God who is our hope and guide
my faithful heart is given,
who lowly stoops to fill my cup
and raise his humble servant up.
God's will this day
I shall obey
rejoicing:
then let the nations sing,
such love and mercy voicing,
and praise their Lord and King.

*Michael Perry (born 1942), from the Latin*

# Donkey Plod and Mary Ride

Donkey plod and Mary ride,
weary Joseph walk beside,
theirs the way that all men come,
dark the night and far from home—

*down the years remember them,*
*come away to Bethlehem.*

Mary's child, on Christmas Eve,
none but ox and ass receive;
theirs the manger and the stall
where is laid the Lord of all—

*down the years remember them,*
*come away to Bethlehem.*

Angels throng the midnight sky:
'Glory be to God on high.'
Theirs the song that sounds abroad,
'Born a Saviour, Christ the Lord'—

*down the years remember them,*
*come away to Bethlehem.*

Shepherds haste the watch to keep
where their Maker lies asleep;
theirs the angels' promised sign,
'Born for us a child divine'—

*down the years remember them,*
*come away to Bethlehem.*

Ancient kings from eastern skies
trace the way of all the wise,
theirs the shining star, to find
light to lighten all mankind—

*down the years remember them,*
*come away to Bethlehem.*

Shepherds, kings and angel throngs,
teach us where our joy belongs:
souls restored and sins forgiven,
Christ on earth the hope of heaven—

*down the years rejoice in them,*
*come away to Bethlehem.*

*Timothy Dudley-Smith (born 1926)*

# THE ROAD TO BETHLEHEM

Clip-clop, clip-clop, slowly the donkey plodded forwards. Joseph walked beside him holding the bridle, trudging through the dusty twilight. It had been a long day and a long journey—but there at last were the roofs of Bethlehem.

Joseph's thoughts went back to that night, months ago now, when first the angel of God had spoken to him in a dream and told him that his wife Mary was to have a son. He was to be named Jesus (which means saviour) because, said the angel, 'he shall save his people from their sins'.

Mary too had had a visitor. The angel Gabriel, one of God's heavenly messengers, had come to stand beside her bed one night.

'Do not be afraid,' Gabriel had said. 'God loves you dearly. You are going to be the mother of a son, and you will call him Jesus. He will be great and will be known as the Son of God Most High. He will be King over Israel for ever; his reign shall never end.'

The donkey stumbled on the stones. Joseph glanced up at Mary and she smiled back—not far to go now. Really, thought Joseph, she shouldn't be making this journey; the baby would come very soon. But the government had ordered everyone to make the journey to the place of their birth to be counted and registered and to pay their taxes. So here they were.

Bethlehem was noisy and full of people. They had nowhere to sleep, and there was no room at the inn; every corner was full of visitors. The best they could do was to find a stable with an empty stall. At last Mary and Joseph, and no doubt the donkey, would have a bite of supper.

And there was one thing more. By the light of the tiny lantern Mary found an empty manger, the wood old and worn, but solid and strong. She and Joseph filled it with the cleanest of the straw, and then there was nothing left to do. The noise of the town died away. Only Mary and Joseph watched and waited, holding hands in the darkness while the oxen munched and snorted in the stalls nearby.

God and his angels kept watch over the darkened stable. It was Christmas Eve.

*Retold from Luke's Gospel, chapters 1 and 2*

# The Stork Carol

The stork she rose on Christmas Eve and said unto her brood,
'I now must go to Bethlehem to see the Son of God.'
She gave to each his dole of meat, she stowed them fairly in
And far she flew and fast she flew and came to Bethlehem.

'Now where is he of David's line?' she asked at house and hall.
'He is not here,' they spoke hardly, 'but in a manger stall.'
She found him in a manger stall with that most holy maid,
The gentle stork she wept to see her Lord so rudely laid.

Then from her panting breast she plucked the feathers white and warm.
She laid them in a manger bed to keep the Lord from harm.
'Now blessed be the gentle stork for evermore,' quoth he,
'For that she saw my sad estate and showed such pity.'

*Anonymous*

# Child in the Manger

Child in the manger, infant of Mary,
Outcast and stranger, Lord of all!
Child who inherits all our transgressions,
All our demerits on him fall.

Once the most holy child of salvation
Gentle and lowly lived below:
Now as our glorious mighty redeemer,
See him victorious o'er each foe.

Prophets foretold him, infant of wonder;
Angels behold him on his throne:
Worthy our Saviour of all their praises;
Happy for ever are his own.

*After Mary MacDonald (1789–1872)*
*L. Macbean (1853-1931)*

14

# Holy Child

Holy child, how still you lie!
safe the manger, soft the hay;
faint upon the eastern sky
breaks the dawn of Christmas Day.

Holy child, whose birthday brings
shepherds from their field and fold,
angel choirs and eastern kings,
myrrh and frankincense and gold:

Holy child, what gift of grace
from the Father freely willed!
In your infant form we trace
all God's promises fulfilled.

Holy child, whose human years
span like ours delight and pain;
one in human joys and tears,
one in all but sin and stain:

Holy child, so far from home,
sons of men to seek and save,
to what dreadful death you come,
to what dark and silent grave!

Holy child, before whose Name
powers of darkness faint and fall;
conquered, death and sin and shame—
Jesus Christ is Lord of all!

Holy child, how still you lie!
safe the manger, soft the hay;
clear upon the eastern sky
breaks the dawn of Christmas Day.

*Timothy Dudley-Smith (born 1926)*

# Away in a Manger

Away in a manger, no crib for a bed,
The little Lord Jesus laid down his sweet head;
The stars in the bright sky looked down where he lay,
The little Lord Jesus asleep on the hay.

The cattle are lowing, the baby awakes,
But little Lord Jesus no crying he makes;
I love thee, Lord Jesus: look down from the sky
And stay by my side until morning is nigh.

Be near me, Lord Jesus: I ask thee to stay
Close by me for ever and love me I pray;
Bless all the dear children in thy tender care,
And fit us for heaven, to live with thee there.

*Verses 1 and 2: anonymous (19th century)*
*Verse 3: J. T. MacFarland (1906)*

*W. J. Kirkpatrick*

# See Him Lying on a Bed of Straw

See him lying on a bed of straw:
a draughty stable with an open door;
Mary cradling the babe she bore—
the prince of glory is his name.

*O now carry me to Bethlehem*
*to see the Lord appear to men*
*just as poor as was the stable then,*
*the prince of glory when he came.*

Star of silver, sweep across the skies,
show where Jesus in the manger lies;
shepherds, swiftly from your stupor rise
to see the saviour of the world!

*Repeat chorus.*

Angels, sing again the song you sang,
bring God's glory to the heart of man;
sing that Bethl'em's little baby can
be salvation to the soul.

*Repeat chorus.*

Mine are riches, from your poverty;
from your innocence, eternity;
mine, forgiveness by your death for me,
child of sorrow for my joy.

*Repeat chorus.*

*Michael Perry (born 1942)*

*Michael Perry*

# Sleep Little Jesus

L ullaby, Jesus, my dear one, be sleeping,
 Lullaby, Jesus, while watch I am keeping.

Hush, he is sleeping while star shines above us,
Like the bright sun is my sweet baby Jesus.

Lullaby, baby, my darling I love you,
Your mother will sing and gently will rock you.

*Traditional Polish*

# He is Born

In a manger he is lying
  Let us go to greet the child!
Baby darling, infant Jesus
Little Saviour sweet and mild;
Bells are ringing, good news bringing,
Join the happy, joyous singing,
'He is born! Oh holy child!'

While the shepherds watch were keeping
Over sheep that starry night,
Angels came and brought good tidings
In a blaze of shining light!
All the shepherds, gently piping,
Ran to see him, softly singing,
'He is born, Oh holy night!'

*Traditional Polish (13th century)*

# How Faint the Stable-Lantern's Light

Ĥow faint the stable-lantern's light
but in the East afar
upon the darkness burning bright
there shines a single star.

A homeless child is brought to birth,
yet love and faith shall find
a candle lit for all the earth,
the hope of humankind;

A flame to warm the barren hearth,
a lamp for all who roam,
to shine upon the heavenward path
and light our journey home.

*Timothy Dudley-Smith (born 1926)*

# Within a Crib

Within a crib my Saviour lay,
a wooden manger filled with hay,
come down for love on Christmas Day:
  all glory be to Jesus!

Upon a cross my Saviour died,
to ransom sinners crucified,
his loving arms still open wide:
  all glory be to Jesus!

A victor's crown my Saviour won,
his work of love and mercy done,
the Father's high-ascended Son:
  all glory be to Jesus!

*Timothy Dudley-Smith (born 1926)*

# Not in Lordly State and Splendour

Not in lordly state and splendour,
  lofty pomp and high renown;
infant-form his robe most royal,
  lantern-light his only crown;
see the new-born King of glory,
  Lord of all to earth come down!

His no rich and storied mansion,
  kingly rule and sceptred sway;
from his seat in highest heaven
  throned among the beasts he lay;
see the new-born King of glory
  cradled in his couch of hay!

Yet the eye of faith beholds him,
  King above all earthly kings;
Lord of uncreated ages,
  he whose praise eternal rings—
see the new-born King of glory
  panoplied by angels' wings!

Not in lordly state and splendour,
  lofty pomp and high renown;
infant-form his robe most royal,
  lantern-light his only crown;
Christ the new-born King of glory,
  Lord of all to earth come down!

*Timothy Dudley-Smith (born 1926)*

# In the Bleak Mid-Winter

In the bleak mid-winter frosty wind made moan,
Earth stood hard as iron, water like a stone;
Snow had fallen, snow on snow, snow on snow,
In the bleak mid-winter, long ago.

Enough for him, whom cherubim worship night and day,
A breastful of milk, and a mangerful of hay;
Enough for him, whom angels fall down before,
The ox and ass and camel which adore.

What can I give him, poor as I am?
If I were a shepherd I would bring a lamb;
If I were a wise man I would do my part;
Yet what I can I give him—give my heart.

*Christina Rossetti (1830–94)*

*G. Holst*

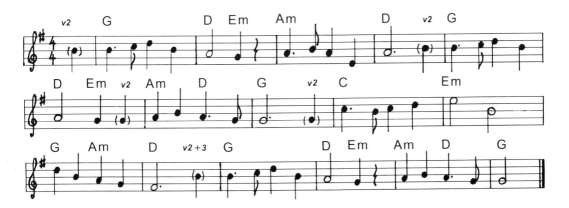

# The Friendly Beasts

Jesus our brother kind and good,
  Was humbly born in a stable rude,
The friendly beasts around him stood,
Jesus our brother kind and good.

'I,' said the donkey all shaggy and brown,
'I carried his mother up hill and down,
I carried her safely to Bethlehem town,'
'I,' said the donkey all shaggy and brown.

'I,' said the cow, all white and red,
'I gave him my manger for a bed,
I gave him my hay to pillow his head,'
'I,' said the cow all white and red.

'I,' said the sheep with the curly horn,
'I gave him my wool for a blanket warm,
He wore my coat on Christmas morn,'
'I,' said the sheep with the curly horn.

'I,' said the dove from the rafters high,
'I cooed him to sleep so he would not cry,
We cooed him to sleep my mate and I,'
'I,' said the dove from the rafters high.

So every beast, by some good spell,
In the stable rude was glad to tell
Of the gift he gave Immanuel,
The gift he gave Immanuel.

*Traditional English (12th century)*

# The Shining Stars Unnumbered

The shining stars unnumbered
on Bethlehem looked down;
unnumbered too the travellers
who thronged to David's town;
no place to rest, no room to spare,
but what the ox and ass may share
for Mary's Son so tender;
she laid him in a manger there,
the Crown of heaven's splendour!

While earth lies hushed and sleeping
nor dreams of Jesus' birth,
hushed deep in new-born slumbers
lies he who made the earth;
and from that stable through the night
there shines a lantern burning bright,
a sign for mortals' seeing,
that Christ is come, the Light of light,
the Lord of all our being!

A sound of angels singing
the watching shepherds heard;
our songs of praise are bringing
anew the promised word;
so let all hearts be joyful when
we hear what angels carolled then
and tell the Christmas story,
of peace on earth, goodwill to men,
through Christ the King of glory!

*Timothy Dudley-Smith (born 1926)*

# The Rocking Carol

Little Jesus, sweetly sleep, do not stir;
We will lend you a coat of fur.
We will rock you, rock you, rock you,
We will rock you, rock you, rock you:
See the fur to keep you warm,
Snugly round your tiny form.

Mary's little baby, sleep, sweetly sleep;
Sleep in comfort, slumber deep.
We will rock you, rock you, rock you,
We will rock you, rock you, rock you:
We will serve you all we can,
Darling, darling little man.

*Traditional Czech*

*Traditional Czech*

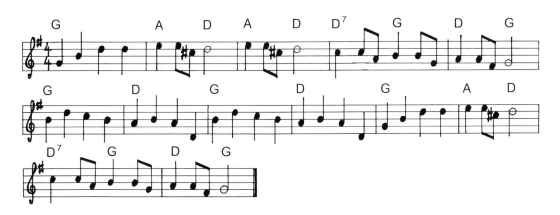

# CHRISTMAS DAY

Out in the fields a wood fire was burning. It had been a big bright blaze at nightfall, but now it was only red embers and sparks dancing in the wind. Beyond the circle of firelight the hills were black under the stars; the sheep were just grey shapes in the darkness, and some of the shepherds were sleeping. A little way below them the townspeople of Bethlehem slept as well.

Suddenly an angel of the Lord appeared among the startled shepherds. Light burst upon them, blazing with the glory of God and the brightness of heaven. The shepherds gazed wide-eyed and open-mouthed, motionless with terror.

'Do not be afraid,' said the angel. 'I bring good news. Today in Bethlehem a saviour has been born for you. He is Christ, the Lord. And this is your sign—you will find a baby lying in a manger.'

And all at once the night sky above them was full of singing angels, praising God and saying: 'Glory to God in highest heaven, and on earth peace for men on whom his favour rests.'

And then once more the shepherds were alone. Darkness and silence settled again on the hills. The fire crackled softly and a sheepbell tinkled. No one spoke or moved. Later the shepherds found themselves hurrying together down the path towards the town. 'A child in a manger,' they thought; and the place to look for a manger is a cowshed or a stable.

Perhaps it was Mary's lantern that brought them to the doorway in the hours before the dawn. All her life long Mary must have remembered those first visitors to her new baby—rough, bearded weather-beaten faces, patched cloaks and stout staffs, strong hands and huge beside baby hands, and eyes still full of the angel's glory.

Soon dawn came to Bethlehem, and then full day. There were no cards and no presents, no decorations, no special food. But there was good news, singing and great joy, and the birth of Jesus.

It was a very happy Christmas!

*Retold from Luke's Gospel, chapter 2*

# Winds Through the Olive Trees

Winds through the olive trees
Softly did blow,
round little Bethlehem
long, long ago.

Sheep on the hillsides lay,
white as the snow;
shepherds were watching them
long, long ago.

Then from the happy skies
angels bent low
singing their songs of joy
long, long ago:

For, in his manger bed
cradled, we know,
Christ came to Bethlehem
long, long ago.

*Traditional French (origin unknown)*

*Traditional French*

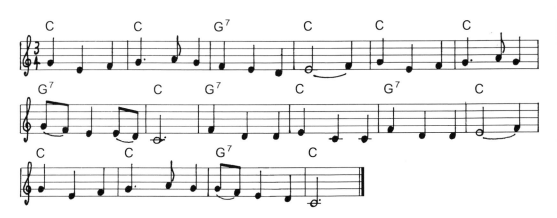

# When Shepherds Watched and Angels Sang

When shepherds watched and angels sang
and Judah's hills with glory rang,
then Christ was born the Son of Man
on Christmas Day in the morning:
Christ was born the Son of man
on Christmas Day, on Christmas Day;
Christ was born the Son of Man
on Christmas Day in the morning.

Where Joseph knelt and Mary bowed
and beasts of burden brayed aloud,
there Christ was born for all our good
on Christmas Day in the morning:
Christ was born for all our good
on Christmas Day, on Christmas Day,
Christ was born for all our good
on Christmas Day in the morning.

When wise men sought and Herod feared
and when a royal star appeared,
then Christ was born to be our Lord
on Christmas Day in the morning:
Christ was born to be our Lord
on Christmas Day, on Christmas Day;
Christ was born to be our Lord
on Christmas Day in the morning.

Where God no longer calls in vain
and human hearts are love's domain,
there Christ is born in us again
on Christmas Day in the morning:
Christ is born in us again
on Christmas Day, on Christmas Day;
Christ is born in us again
on Christmas Day in the morning.

*Michael Perry (born 1942)*

# While Shepherds Watched Their Flocks by Night

While shepherds watched their flocks by night,
All seated on the ground,
The angel of the Lord came down,
And glory shone around.

'Fear not,' said he, (for mighty dread
Had seized their troubled mind),
'Glad tidings of great joy I bring
To you and all mankind.

'To you in David's town this day
Is born of David's line
A saviour, who is Christ the Lord;
And this shall be the sign:

The heavenly babe you there shall find
To human view displayed,
All meanly wrapped in swathing bands,
And in a manger laid.'

*Nahum Tate (1652-1715)*

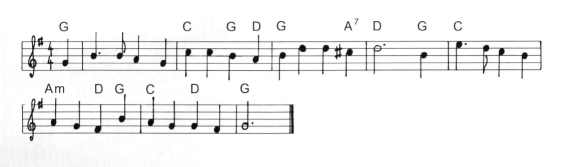

# O Little Town of Bethlehem

O little town of Bethlehem,
  How still we see thee lie!
Above thy deep and dreamless sleep
The silent stars go by:
Yet in thy dark streets shineth
The everlasting Light;
The hopes and fears of all the years
Are met in thee tonight.

O morning stars, together
Proclaim the holy birth,
And praises sing to God the King,
And peace to men on earth.
For Christ is born of Mary
And, gathered all above,
While mortals sleep, the angels keep
Their watch of wondering love.

O holy child of Bethlehem,
Descend to us, we pray:
Cast out our sin, and enter in,
Be born in us today.
We hear the Christmas angels
The great glad tidings tell:
O come to us, abide with us,
Our Lord Emmanuel.

*Bishop Phillips Brooks (1835–93)*

*Traditional English*

# Stars of Heaven Clear and Bright

Stars of heaven, clear and bright,
shine upon this Christmas night.
Vaster far than midnight skies
are its timeless mysteries.
Trampled earth and stable floor
lift the heart to heaven's door—

*God has sent to us his Son,*
*earth and heaven meet as one.*

Sleepy sounds of beast and byre
mingle with the angel choir.
Highest heaven bends in awe
where he lies amid the straw,
who from light eternal came
aureoled in candle-flame—

*God has sent to us his Son,*
*earth and heaven meet as one.*

Wide-eyed shepherds mutely gaze
at the child whom angels praise.
Threefold gifts the wise men bring,
to the infant priest and king:
to the Lord immortal, myrrh
for an earthly sepulchre—

*God has sent to us his Son,*
*earth and heaven meet as one.*

Heaven of heavens hails his birth,
King of glory, child of earth,
born in flesh to reign on high,
Prince of life to bleed and die.
Throned on Mary's lap he lies,
Lord of all eternities—

*God has sent to us his Son,*
*earth and heaven meet as one.*

'Glory be to God on high,
peace on earth,' the angels cry.
Ancient enmities at rest,
ransomed, reconciled and blest,
in the peace of Christ we come,
come we joyful, come we home—

*God has sent to us his Son,*
*earth and heaven meet as one.*

*Timothy Dudley-Smith (born 1926)*

# Angels From the Realms of Glory

Angels from the realms of glory
Wing your flight o'er all the earth;
Ye, who sang creation's story
Now proclaim Messiah's birth:

*Come and worship,*
*Christ the new-born King,*
*Come and worship,*
*Worship Christ, the new-born King.*

Shepherds in their fields abiding,
Watching o'er your flocks by night,
God with man is now residing,
Yonder shines the infant Light:

*Repeat chorus.*

Saints before the altar bending,
Watching long in hope and fear,
Suddenly the Lord, descending,
In his temple shall appear:

*Repeat chorus.*

*James Montgomery (1771-1854)*

# The Holly and the Ivy

The holly and the ivy,
 When they are both full grown,
Of all the trees that are in the wood,
The holly bears the crown.

 *O the rising of the sun*
 *And the running of the deer,*
 *The playing of the merry organ,*
 *Sweet singing in the choir.*

The holly bears a blossom
As white as the lily flower,
And Mary bore sweet Jesus Christ
To be our sweet Saviour.

 *Repeat chorus.*

The holly bears a berry
As red as any blood,
And Mary bore sweet Jesus Christ
To do poor sinners good.

 *Repeat chorus.*

The holly bears a prickle
As sharp as any thorn,
And Mary bore sweet Jesus Christ
On Christmas Day in the morn.

 *Repeat chorus.*

The holly bears a bark,
As bitter as any gall,
And Mary bore sweet Jesus Christ
For to redeem us all.

 *Repeat chorus.*

*Traditional English*

*Traditional English*

# The Colours of Christmas

Blue was the colour that sweet Mary wore,
Brown were the oxen asleep in the straw,
Black was the sky on that cold winter's night,
But gold was the star that was shining so bright,
Gold was the star that was shining so bright.

Grey was the donkey asleep in the stall,
Purple the wise men so grave and so tall,
Silver the three kings who rode through the night,
But gold was the star that was shining so bright,
Gold was the star that was shining so bright.

Gold was the baby who came down to earth,
Gold was the angel who told of his birth,
Gold was the sky on that glorious night,
And gold was the star that was shining so bright,
Gold was the star that was shining so bright.

*S. Stevens*

# Silent Night

Silent night! Holy night!
All is calm, all is bright,
Round yon virgin mother and child;
Holy infant, so tender and mild,
Sleep in heavenly peace,
Sleep in heavenly peace.

Silent night! Holy night!
Shepherds quail at the sight;
Glories stream from heaven afar,
Heavenly hosts sing Alleluia!
Christ the Saviour is born,
Christ the Saviour is born.

Silent night! Holy night!
Son of God, love's pure light
Radiant beams thy holy face,
With the dawn of redeeming grace,
Jesus, Lord, at thy birth,
Jesus, Lord, at thy birth.

*Joseph Mohr (1792-1848)*
*translated by John Freeman Young (1820-85)*

*Franz Grüber*

# I Saw Three Ships

I saw three ships come sailing in,
On Christmas Day, on Christmas Day
I saw three ships come sailing in,
On Christmas Day in the morning.

And what was in those ships all three,
On Christmas Day, on Christmas Day
And what was in those ships all three,
On Christmas Day in the morning.

The virgin Mary and Christ were there,
On Christmas Day, on Christmas day
The virgin Mary and Christ were there,
On Christmas Day in the morning.

Pray whither sailed those ships all three?
On Christmas Day, on Christmas Day
Pray whither sailed those ships all three?
On Christmas Day in the morning.

O they sailed into Bethlehem,
On Christmas Day, on Christmas Day
O they sailed into Bethlehem,
On Christmas Day in the morning.

And all the bells on earth shall ring
On Christmas Day, on Christmas Day
And all the bells on earth shall ring
On Christmas Day in the morning.

*Traditional English*

*Traditional English*

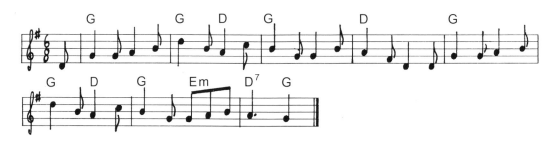

# The Carol of the Birds

From out of a wood did a cuckoo fly, cuckoo,
   He came to a manger with joyful cry, cuckoo.
He hopped, he curtsied, round he flew,
And loud his jubilation grew.
Cuckoo, cuckoo, cuckoo.

A pigeon flew over to Galilee, coo—oo,
He strutted and cooed and was full of glee, coo—oo,
And showed with jewelled wings unfurled,
His joy that Christ was in the world,
Coo—oo, coo—oo, coo—oo.

A dove settled down upon Nazareth, toucroo,
And tenderly chanted with all his breath, toucroo.
'Oh you,' he cooed, 'so good and true,
My beauty do I give to you—
Toucroo, toucroo, toucroo.'

*Traditional Czech*

# WISE MEN FROM THE EAST

Clearly, they had come a long way. You could see that from their luggage, their jars, pouches and leather bags; and from their strange clothes and high-boned foreign faces.

These strange foreign visitors were wise men from the east. They had seen a new star in the night sky, far away in their own country, and according to their books and legends it was the sign of a king's birth—a very great king indeed. The star called them to leave their homes and make the journey to find the king; and they had precious gifts in their saddlebags.

Travel-worn and tired, they had come at last to the city of Jerusalem, where the cruel King Herod reigned. Now he knew nothing of the birth of any other king nearby. But his advisers told him of an ancient promise in the scroll of the prophet Micah that the King of Israel would be born in Bethlehem, just a few miles away.

Cunningly Herod sent the wise men to Bethlehem, saying, 'When you have found your new king, come back and tell me, so that I may go myself and worship him.' But in his wicked heart he planned to kill the child and so be free of any rivals to his throne.

So the wise men set off on their camels. The star which they had seen in the East still went in front of them, until at last it shone directly over the house where Mary and Joseph were lodging with their son. The foreigners dismounted and fell on their knees to worship Jesus. They had found the king they had come so far to seek.

One by one they gave to Mary the gifts they had brought for Jesus: gold, precious and glinting in the lamplight; and spices, filling the room with the heavy fragrance of frankincense and myrrh.

They left as mysteriously as they came; but they did not go back to Herod as God warned them in dream that Herod was not to be trusted.

But among the clothes and blankets Mary kept for Jesus, there remained the strange rich gifts by which she would always remember the strangers— yellow gold, sweet-smelling frankincense, and bitter myrrh.

*Retold from Matthew's Gospel, chapter 2*

# See Amid the Winter's Snow

See amid the winter's snow,
Born for us on earth below,
See the tender Lamb appears,
Promised from eternal years.

*Hail, thou ever-blessed morn!*
*Hail, redemption's happy dawn!*
*Sing through all Jerusalem:*
*Christ is born in Bethlehem!*

Lo, within a manger lies
He who built the starry skies;
He, who throned in heights sublime,
Sits among the cherubim!

*Repeat chrorus.*

Say, ye holy shepherds, say,
What your joyful news today?
Wherefore have ye left your sheep
On the lonely mountain steep?

*Repeat chorus.*

'As we watched at dead of night,
Lo, we saw a wondrous light;
Angels singing peace on earth
Told us of the Saviour's birth.'

*Repeat chorus.*

Sacred infant, all-divine,
What a tender love was thine
Thus to come from highest bliss
Down to such a world as this!

*Repeat chorus.*

*E. Caswall (1814–78)*

*John Goss*

# There Were Three Kings

There were three kings on a journey did go,
Led by a star through the cold winter's deep snow.
Joyfully they came on their way
Searching for him who was born King on that day.
With drums and with trumpets they came on their way.
An angel came, to Joseph did say
'Oh hurry to Egypt! Go! Please don't delay;
Herod comes near, vengeance to reap.
So hurry now, hasten, and Mary don't weep.'
On donkey they went with sweet Jesus asleep,
Cradled by Mary, sweet Jesus did sleep.

*Traditional Flemish*

# Who is He in Yonder Stall?

Who is he in yonder stall
At whose feet the shepherds fall?
'Tis the Lord—O, wondrous story!
'Tis the Lord, the King of glory!
At his feet we humbly fall—
Crown him, crown him Lord of all.

*B. R. Hanby (1833–1867)*

# A Song was Heard at Christmas

A song was heard at Christmas
  to wake the midnight sky;
a Saviour's birth, and peace on earth,
  and praise to God on high.
The angels sang at Christmas
  with all the hosts above,
and still we sing the newborn King,
  his glory and his love.

A star was seen at Christmas,
  a herald and a sign,
that all might know the way to go
  to find the child divine.
The wise men watched at Christmas
  in some far eastern land,
and still the wise in starry skies
  discern their Maker's hand.

A tree was grown at Christmas,
  a sapling green and young;
no tinsel bright with candlelight
  upon its branches hung.
But he who came at Christmas
  our sins and sorrows bore,
and still we name his tree of shame
  our life for evermore.

A child was born at Christmas
  when Christmas first began;
the Lord of all a baby small,
  for love of men made man.
For love is ours at Christmas,
  and life and light restored,
and so we praise through endless days
  The Saviour, Christ the Lord.

*Timothy Dudley-Smith (born 1926)*

# We Three Kings

We three kings of Orient are;
Bearing gifts we traverse afar
Field and fountain, moor and mountain
Following yonder star.

*O star of wonder, star of night,*
*Star with royal beauty bright,*
*Westward leading, still proceeding,*
*Guide us to thy perfect light.*


Born a King on Bethlehem's plain
Gold I bring to crown him again;
King for ever, ceasing never,
Over us all to reign.

*Repeat chorus.*

Frankincense to offer have I,
Incense owns a deity nigh;
Prayer and praising, all men raising,
Worship him, God most high.

*Repeat chorus.*

Myrrh is mine; its bitter perfume
Breathes a life of gathering gloom;
Sorrowing, sighing, bleeding, dying
Sealed in the stone-cold tomb.

*Repeat chorus.*

Glorious now behold Him arise—
King and God and sacrifice!
Heaven sings 'Alleluia!'
'Alleluia!' the earth replies.

*Repeat chorus.*

*John Henry Hopkins (1820–91)*

*John Henry Hopkins*

# The Golden Carol

The star we've waited for so long
To tell us of his coming,
Is here! Is here! And we must go
With trumpets and drums drumming!
The star we follow on this night
Will lead us to the cradle,
Where he was born this holy night
In poor and lowly stable.

The way is long, the way is cold,
We cannot tarry longer,
The birth of him the star has told
The way is still much longer.
A king is born this holy morn
And gifts to him we're bringing.
The child we've waited for is born!
Oh hear the angels singing!

*Traditional English*

# Joy to the World

Joy to the world! the Lord is come;
Let earth receive her King;
Let ev'ry heart prepare him room,
And heaven and nature sing,
And heaven and nature sing,
And heaven and nature sing.

Joy to the world! the Saviour reigns;
Let men their songs employ;
While fields and floods, rocks, hills
 and plains
Repeat the sounding joy,
Repeat the sounding joy,
Repeat, repeat the sounding joy.

He rules the world with truth and grace,
And makes the nations prove
The glories of his righteousness,
And wonders of his love,
And wonders of his love,
And wonders, and wonders of his love.

*I. Watts (1674–1748)*

# Now Light One Thousand Christmas Lights

Now light one thousand Christmas lights
   On dark earth here tonight;
One thousand, thousand also shine
To make the dark sky bright.

Oh, once when skies were starry bright,
In stable cold and bare,
Sweet Mary bore a son that night.
A child both kind and fair.

He came to bring us love and light
To bring us peace on earth,
So let your candles shine tonight
And sing with joy and mirth.

*Traditional Swedish*

# O Come Little Children

O come little children, O come one and all!
O come to the cradle in Bethlehem's stall,
The bright star will guide us and show us the way
To Jesus who's lying asleep on the hay.

The animals all seem to know Mary's boy
And Joseph, with Mary, beholds him with joy;
The shepherds have entered, to him love they bring,
While angels sing joyously, merrily sing.

O come with the shepherds, O come to the stall
With hearts full of love for the one who loves all;
O sing, little children to him you adore,
Sing with the angels, sing peace evermore.

*Christoph von Schmid (1768–1854)*

*Johann A. P. Schulz (1747–1800)*

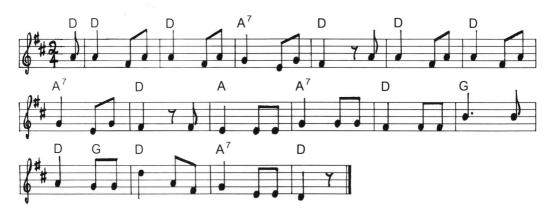

# Christmas Day is Come

Christmas Day is come; let's all prepare for mirth,
  With songs of joy and gladness, for Christ is come to earth.
Here within the stable the new-born baby lies,
For him sing all the angels; their singing fills the skies.
They hail with adoration, 'All holy' do they cry,
They sing 'Hosanna, holy, holy infant' on high.

Holy maid and baby in the stable cold and bare;
But where is there a palace that could with this compare?
Mary is the queen in heaven and on earth,
Her son is King of Kings—to him she did give birth.
He comes to live among us, to bring us peace and love;
To show us we are brothers both here and above.

*Traditional Irish (17th century)*

# The Sussex Carol

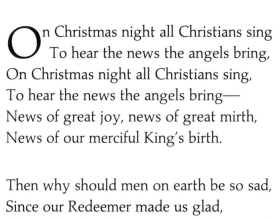

On Christmas night all Christians sing
  To hear the news the angels bring,
On Christmas night all Christians sing,
To hear the news the angels bring—
News of great joy, news of great mirth,
News of our merciful King's birth.

Then why should men on earth be so sad,
Since our Redeemer made us glad,
Then why should men on earth be so sad,
Since our Redeemer made us glad,
When from our sin he set us free
All for to gain our liberty?

All out of darkness we have light,
Which made the angels sing this night;
All out of darkness we have light,
Which made the angels sing this night:
'Glory to God and peace to men
Now and for evermore. Amen.'

*Traditional English*

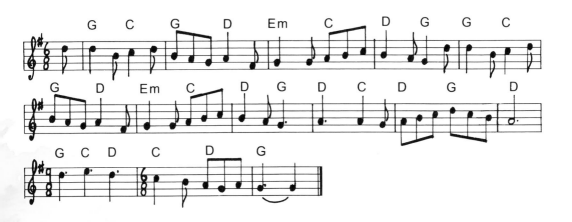

# Merry Christmas

Merry Christmas, Merry Christmas and a Happy New Year
To Father and Mother and everyone here!

*Repeat*

'Twas in Bethlehem's city that Jesus was born
A star it was shining, both evening and morn.

*Repeat*

Oh, I wish we could follow that star on this day
For all the way to heaven it lightens our way.

*Repeat*

*Traditional Swedish*

*Traditional Swedish*

58

# Come Now with Awe

Come now with awe, earth's ancient vigil keeping;
cold under starlight lies the stony way.
Down from the hillside see the shepherds creeping,
hear in our hearts the whispered news they say:
    'Laid in a manger lies an infant sleeping,
    Christ our Redeemer, born for us today.'

Come now with joy to worship and adore him;
hushed in the stillness, wonder and behold—
Christ in the stable where his mother bore him,
Christ whom the prophets faithfully foretold:
    High King of ages, low we kneel before him,
    starlight for silver, lantern-light for gold.

Come now with faith, the age-long secret guessing,
hearts rapt in wonder, soul and spirit stirred—
see in our likeness love beyond expressing,
all God has spoken, all the prophets heard;
    born for us sinners, bearer of all blessing,
    flesh of our flesh, behold the eternal Word!

Come now with love; beyond our comprehending
love in its fulness lies in mortal span!
How should we love, whom Love is so befriending?
Love rich in mercy since our race began
    now stoops to save us, sighs and sorrows ending,
    Jesus our Saviour, Son of God made man.

*Timothy Dudley-Smith (born 1926)*

# Hark! the Herald Angels Sing

Hark! the herald angels sing,
'Glory to the new-born King,
Peace on earth, and mercy mild,
God and sinners reconciled.'
Joyful, all ye nations rise,
Join the triumph of the skies;
With the angelic host proclaim,
'Christ is born in Bethlehem.'

*Hark! the herald angels sing*
*'Glory to the new-born King.'*

Christ, by highest heaven adored,
Christ, the everlasting Lord,
Late in time behold him come,
Offspring of a virgin's womb.
Veiled in flesh the Godhead see!
Hail the incarnate Deity!
Pleased as man with man to dwell,
Jesus, our Emmanuel.

*Repeat chorus.*

Hail, the heaven-born Prince of Peace!
Hail, the Sun of Righteousness!
Light and life to all he brings,
Risen with healing in his wings.
Mild he lays his glory by,
Born that man no more may die,
Born to raise the sons of earth;
Born to give them second birth.

*Repeat chorus.*

*Charles Wesley (1707–88)*

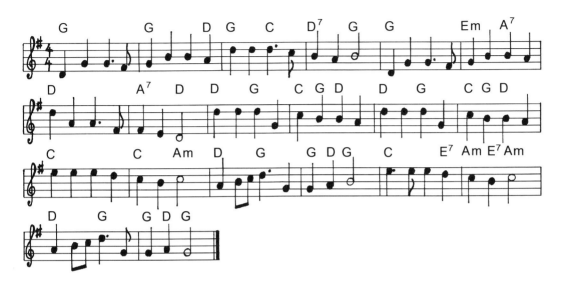